KIDS CAN COOK!

GRILL MASTER

FINGER-LICKING GRILLED RECIPES

BY TYLER OMOTH

CAPSTONE PRESS
a capstone imprint

Edge Books are published by Capstone Press,
1710 Roe Crest Drive, North Mankato, Minnesota 56003
www.mycapstone.com

Library of Congress Cataloging-in-Publication Data
Names: Omoth, Tyler, author.
Title: Grill master : finger-licking grilled recipes / by Tyler Omoth.
Description: Mankato, Minnesota : Capstone Press, [2017] | Series: Edge books.
   Kids can cook! | Audience: Ages 10-13. | Audience: Grades 4-6. |
   Includes bibliographical references.
Identifiers: LCCN 2016028373 (print) | LCCN 2016031737 (ebook) |
   ISBN 9781515738152 (library binding) | ISBN 9781515738275 (eBook PDF)
Subjects: LCSH: Barbecuing—Juvenile literature. | Outdoor cooking—Juvenile
   literature. | LCGFT: Cookbooks.
Classification: LCC TX840.B3 O46 2017 (print) | LCC TX840.B3 (ebook) |
   DDC 641.5/784—dc23
LC record available at https://lccn.loc.gov/2016028373

Summary
Easy-to-follow instructions and cooking tips teach young readers how to cook a variety of
amazing grilled recipes.

Editorial Credits
Aaron Sautter, editor; Sarah Bennett, designer; Laura Manthe, production specialist

Photo Credits
All photographs by Capstone Studio/Karon Dubke, Sarah Schuette, Food Stylist

Printed in Canada.
010021S17

TABLE OF CONTENTS

READY, SET, GRILL!

When it comes to summertime eats, nothing beats the finger-licking foods cooked on an outdoor grill. The smells of smoke, roasting meat, and special sauces combine to make people's mouths water and their stomachs growl.

Grilling can be much more than just tossing on some hot dogs or burgers to heat up over the fire. With practice you can make amazing meals like shrimp tacos, bacon-wrapped corn on the cob, and even grilled pizza! And who doesn't love a rack of tender barbecue ribs? They're not only delicious, but can really show off your cooking skills.

Are you ready to amaze your family and friends and make your neighbors hungry? With the following recipes you can do just that. Fire up your grill and get ready to become a grilling master!

SAFETY FIRST

Cooking on a grill can be a lot of fun, but working around hot flames can be dangerous too. It's important to keep safety in mind at all times when you're grilling your food. Here are a few tips to remember to stay safe.

- Tie back long hair and tuck in loose clothing to avoid catching them on fire. Be extra careful when using cooking oils. If they spill into the fire, it can cause a large and dangerous flare-up.

- Cook with metal utensils. Be careful with tools that have rubber or plastic handles that can melt in the fire.

- Use dry pot holders or oven mitts whenever handling hot cookware or other items.

- Always ask an adult for permission to use sharp knives.

- Always cut your food on a cutting board. Avoid cutting your fingers by holding food with your fingertips curved inward. You should also always make sure that the knife blade points away from your body as you're cutting.

- Avoid spreading germs by washing your hands with soap and warm water. Do this both before and after preparing food.

- Always wash fruits and vegetables before preparing them.

COOKING TIPS AND TRICKS

The best cooks usually have a plan in place before beginning any meal. Follow these tips to cook like a pro.

- Read all the way through a recipe before you begin. Then gather together the equipment and ingredients you'll need to make the recipe.

- Clear your workspace of clutter and keep the surface clean.

- Keep things simple by putting food and ingredients away as you work.

- Stay by the grill while you cook to avoid food disasters.

- Clean up completely when you're done.

MEASUREMENTS	
1/8 teaspoon	0.6 gram or milliliter
1/4 teaspoon	1.25 g or ml
1/2 teaspoon	2.5 g or ml
1 teaspoon	5 g or ml
1 tablespoon	15 g or ml
1/4 cup	57 g (dry) or 60 ml (liquid)
1/3 cup	75 g (dry) or 80 ml (liquid)
1/2 cup	114 g (dry) or 125 ml (liquid)
3/4 cup	170 g (dry) or 175 ml (liquid)
1 cup	227 g (dry) or 240 ml (liquid)
1 quart	950 ml
1 ounce	28 g
1 pound	454 g

PROPERLY MEASURING INGREDIENTS

- If possible, use transparent glass or plastic cups so you can check measurements at eye level.

- Measuring cups with a handle and spout are useful for liquid ingredients.

- Spoon dry ingredients into a measuring cup and level it with a knife.

- Measuring spoons are good for both liquid and dry ingredients.

GRILLING TERMS

baste — to moisten meat or other food with drippings or sauces while cooking

direct heat — food is cooked directly above the heat source

dry rub — a mixture of dry seasonings that is rubbed into meat to add flavor before grilling

flare-up — flames that occur during cooking due to dripping fat or oils

indirect heat — food is cooked away from the heat source

marinade — a sauce used to add flavor and moisture to meat before grilling

medium — warm and pink in the center; cooked to 145° F (63° C)

medium rare — warm and slightly red in the center; cooked to 135° F (57° C)

medium well — hot and only slightly pink in the center; cooked to 150° F (66° C)

propane — a gas used to fuel the fire in gas grills

rare — cooler and red in the center; cooked to 125° F (52° C)

warming rack — the upper rack in a grill, used to keep food warm or cook it more slowly

well done — hot and brown or gray throughout; cooked to 160° F (71° C)

TEMPERATURE

Fahrenheit	Celsius
325°	160°
350°	180°
375°	190°
400°	200°
425°	220°
450°	230°

Add Some Smoke!

One of the best ways to add great aroma and flavor to food is to use smoke in your grilling. Try different types of wood like apple, mesquite, or hickory to discover the flavor you like best. If using a charcoal grill, you can just toss a couple chunks of wood on top of your coals. For a gas grill, make a "smoke bomb" by placing wood chips in an aluminum foil packet. Poke some holes in the foil and place the packet on the grill over the burner. Keep the grill closed to let the smoke surround and penetrate your meat.

USING YOUR GRILL

Charcoal Grills — Charcoal grills can be a little messy, but they give your food great flavor. Charcoal must be burned properly before you can cook over it. First, stack the briquettes on top of crumpled newspaper or use a chimney starter with newspaper at the bottom. Light the newspaper to begin burning the charcoal. Avoid using lighter fluid if possible. It adds an unpleasant chemical odor and flavor to your food. After the coals are gray and hot, use charcoal tongs to spread them evenly or move them to one side for indirect heat.

Gas Grills — Gas grills use propane gas to fuel the flames. Gas grills are cleaner and easier to use than charcoal grills. Many can be lit with the push of a button. Gas grills also make it easy to control the temperature for cooking. However, they don't add as much flavor to your food.

Always keep your gas grill clean to avoid flare-ups. To clean the grill, turn up the heat to burn off excess grease and stuck-on food. Then scrub the grates clean with a wire brush or crumpled up aluminum foil.

GRILLING TOOLS

Rib Rack — This wire rack is specially designed to hold several racks of ribs upright in the grill. The design allows smoke to flow around the ribs and penetrate the meat.

Meat Thermometer — A thermometer that is poked into the center of cooking meats to determine internal temperature.

Wire Grill Brush — A good grill brush is a must-have for every grill master. Keeping the grill clean is important for safety and to get the best flavor from your food.

Tongs — Tongs work great for picking up and flipping things like hot dogs, bratwurst, and chicken.

Sharp Knives — Using dull, old knives makes it harder to cut things like potatoes or meat. Properly sharpened knives make cooking easier, safer, and more fun.

Skewers — Skewers are long, thin rods that you thread through meats and veggies. Skewers can be made of metal or wood. If using wood skewers, soak in water for 30 minutes before using to avoid burning them.

Spatula — Use a long-handled grilling spatula for flipping burgers and other foods. The long handle keeps your hand away from the heat.

CHICKEN ZINGERS

MAKES 8 SERVINGS

Chicken strips are an easy crowd pleaser. How do you make them even better? Add delicious, smoky bacon and cook them on the grill! These tasty finger snacks are awesome for sharing at parties or the big game. Cook them up, grab your favorite dipping sauce, and enjoy!

INGREDIENTS

1 cup of mayonnaise
¼ cup ranch dressing
1 tablespoon honey-dijon mustard
3 pounds of boneless, skinless chicken
    breasts or tenders
1 package of thick-cut bacon

EQUIPMENT

medium bowl
mixing spoon
sharp cooking knife
cutting board
wood toothpicks
cooking tongs

STEPS

1. Mix the mayonnaise, ranch dressing, and mustard together in the bowl.

2. Cut the chicken breasts into 1-inch (2.5-centimeter) wide strips, or use precut chicken tenders.

3. Evenly spread the mayonnaise mixture onto the chicken strips.

4. Cut the bacon strips in half. Wrap one half strip around each coated chicken strip. Insert a wood toothpick through the chicken to hold the bacon in place.

5. Grill over high heat. Place the chicken strips on the grill with the bacon ends down and cook for 5 minutes. Flip the strips over and cook another 5 minutes. Continue to flip and cook until the bacon is crisp and the chicken is lightly browned.

6. Remove the strips from the grill and let them cool for a few minutes. Then remove the toothpicks, serve, and enjoy!

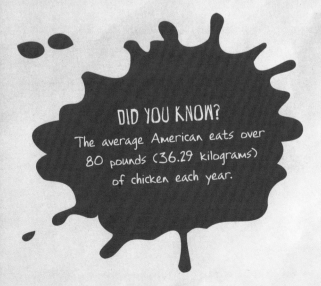

DID YOU KNOW?
The average American eats over 80 pounds (36.29 kilograms) of chicken each year.

BACON-WRAPPED CORN ON THE COB

MAKES 4 EARS OF CORN

Corn on the cob is always a tasty summertime treat. Cook it on the grill, and it becomes extra special and flavorful. But if you add some bacon, suddenly you have a smoky masterpiece that will keep people asking for more!

INGREDIENTS

4 ears of sweet corn, husked
   and cleaned
8 strips of thick-cut bacon
salt
pepper

EQUIPMENT

aluminum foil
cooking tongs

DID YOU KNOW?
Almost every cob of corn has an even number of rows of kernels, never odd.

STEPS

1. Wrap two strips of bacon around each ear of corn.

2. Sprinkle with salt and pepper to your liking.

3. Wrap each ear of corn in aluminum foil. Twist the ends to seal tightly and make handles for turning.

4. Grill over high heat for 10 minutes. Rotate corn two to three times during this step to cook evenly on each side.

5. Reduce heat to low and cook for 35 to 45 minutes, or until the bacon is crisp and the corn is tender.

6. Remove from grill and let cool for a few minutes before unwrapping the foil. Now grab some napkins and chomp away!

SWEET-AND-SOUR KABOBS

MAKES 8 KABOBS

If you're craving something sweet and tangy, these sweet-and-sour kabobs should hit the spot. These easy, sweet and tangy treats make a great appetizer. Or you can add some cooked rice to make a tasty, healthy meal.

INGREDIENTS

2 pounds of skinless, boneless
   chicken breast
1 red bell pepper
1 yellow bell pepper
1 green bell pepper
1 can (20 ounces)
   pineapple chunks
1 jar (11.5 ounces)
   sweet and sour sauce
3 tablespoons vegetable oil

EQUIPMENT

sharp cooking knife
cutting board
large mixing bowl
large mixing spoon
medium mixing bowl
whisk
plastic wrap
8 grilling skewers
cooking tongs
basting brush

STEPS

1 Cut the chicken breasts into 1.5-inch (3.8-cm) cubes and place in the large mixing bowl.

3 Cut each of the peppers in half. Remove all of the seeds and stems. Cut the peppers into 1-inch (2.5-cm) wide pieces and add to mixing bowl.

4 Open and drain the can of pineapple and add to mixing bowl. Stir all the ingredients together.

5 Pour the sweet and sour sauce into the medium bowl. Add the vegetable oil and whisk until well blended.

6 Pour ¾ of the sauce over the vegetables and chicken mixture. Reserve the rest of the sauce for basting later.

7 Stir the vegetables and chicken until everything is coated with the sauce. Cover the bowl with plastic wrap and place in refrigerator. Allow mixture to marinate for at least 2 to 3 hours.

8 When ready to grill, thread the chicken and vegetables onto the skewers. Make them colorful by alternating the green pepper, pineapple, red pepper, chicken, and yellow pepper.

9 Grill on medium-high heat for 12 to 15 minutes, turning often with tongs to cook evenly.

10 Baste one side of the kabobs with leftover sweet and sour sauce. Cook for 2 minutes. Turn the kabobs over and baste the other side with more sauce. Cook for another 1 to 2 minutes.

11 Remove the kabobs from the grill and allow to cool for 2 to 3 minutes before serving.

CHEESY SURPRISE BURGER

MAKES 4 BURGERS

It's a cheese explosion! Instead of slapping a slice of cheese on top of a burger, give your burgers a melty, gooey cheese center. Stuffing the ground beef with golden goodness provides a surprise burst of flavor with every bite.

Try This!

These burgers are great with any of your favorite cheeses. Try provolone, spicy pepper jack, smoked gouda, or other cheeses for some tasty flavor combinations.

INGREDIENTS

1 pound ground beef
¼ teaspoon salt
¼ teaspoon garlic powder
pinch of black pepper
¼ teaspoon Worcestershire sauce
8 slices of Colby Jack or
   American cheese
vegetable or olive oil
4 onion roll buns
lettuce
sliced onions
sliced tomatoes
pickle chips
ketchup, mustard, mayonnaise, or
   your favorite barbeque sauce

EQUIPMENT

medium mixing bowl
large plate
basting brush
grilling spatula
serving platter

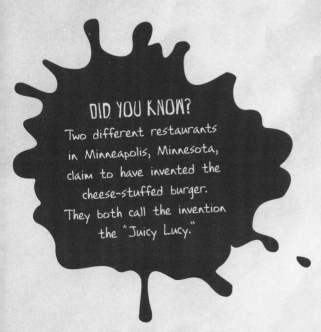

DID YOU KNOW?
Two different restaurants in Minneapolis, Minnesota, claim to have invented the cheese-stuffed burger. They both call the invention the "Juicy Lucy."

STEPS

1 Mix together the ground beef and seasonings in the mixing bowl.

2 Roll the meat into 8 evenly sized balls about 1.5 inches (3.8 cm) in size. Then press into flat patties about 0.25-inch (0.6-cm) thick.

3 Fold each slice of cheese into fourths.

4 Lay out four beef patties on the plate. Place two folded cheese slices at the center of each beef patty.

5 Place the remaining beef patties on top of the patties with cheese. Then press the edges of the patties together to seal in the cheese.

6 Brush the outside of the burgers with oil so they don't stick to the grill.

7 Heat the grill to about 450° F.

8 Add the burgers to the grill and cook for 3 to 4 minutes. Flip them over with a spatula and cook for another 3 to 4 minutes, or to an internal temperature of 140° to 150° F.

9 Remove the burgers to a clean platter and allow them to cool for 2 to 3 minutes.

10 Put each burger on a bun. Then add your favorite toppings and enjoy a delicious burst of cheesy goodness!

HAWAIIAN CHICKEN SANDWICH

MAKES 4 SANDWICHES

Here is a delicious way to make a grilled chicken breast into a fun sandwich. The sweet and smoky teriyaki sauce mixed with the tangy burst of pineapple will make your cookout feel like a Hawaiian luau. Your family will be hula dancing for more!

INGREDIENTS

4 medium-sized boneless,
  skinless chicken breasts
  (fresh or thawed)
1/4 cup pre-made teriyaki sauce
  (plus extra for basting)
1 medium onion
4 teaspoons butter
4 Hawaiian rolls
1 (8-ounce) can of pineapple
  slices, well drained (or fresh
  pineapple slices)
4 slices of provolone, Swiss, or
  mozzarella cheese
4 leaves of green leaf lettuce

EQUIPMENT

sealable plastic bag
sharp cooking knife
cutting board
basting brush
meat thermometer
grilling tongs
butter knife

STEPS

1. Place the chicken breasts in the sealable bag and add the teriyaki sauce. Seal the bag and shake it to coat the chicken with the sauce. Allow the meat to marinate in the bag for at least 30 minutes. Set aside the extra sauce for basting later.

2. Peel the onion and slice into 1/4-inch (0.6-cm) thick slices.

3. Heat the grill to about 350° F.

4. Place chicken breasts on the grill 6 to 8 inches (15 to 20 cm) from the heat source. Cook for 8 to 10 minutes. Brush the chicken with more teriyaki sauce before flipping.

5. Flip the chicken breasts and brush more sauce on the other side. Cook the breasts for another 8 to 10 minutes, or until the center reaches 165° F. The juices from the meat should run clear when pressed.

6. Place the onion slices on the grill. Cook for 4 to 5 minutes or until the onions are soft and brown. Brush on more teriyaki sauce if desired.

7. Spread butter lightly on the Hawaiian rolls. Add to the grill butter-side down, away from the heat source. Cook for 2 minutes or until toasted.

8. Place the pineapple slices on the grill, close to the heat source. Cook for 1 minute per side.

9. Add the cheese slices to the chicken breasts for the last minute of grilling and allow it to melt.

10. When everything is done, pull all the ingredients off the grill. Build the sandwiches using the lettuce. Time to enjoy your Hawaiian treat!

TEX-MEX SHRIMP TACOS

MAKES 6 TACOS

Grilling is a great American tradition, but adding flavors from other cultures adds delicious variety to your cookouts. Shrimp are really easy to cook on the grill and they make great tacos! This recipe is great for adding some south-of-the-border flavor on a fun summer evening with friends or family.

INGREDIENTS

1 pound of large, frozen, raw shrimp
   (peeled and deveined)
2 tablespoons olive oil
1 lime, juiced
1 teaspoon cumin
¼ cup fresh, finely chopped cilantro
½ teaspoon salt
¼ teaspoon pepper
6 medium-sized flour tortillas
toppings such as shredded cabbage,
   chopped tomatoes, avocado, sour
   cream, and salsa

EQUIPMENT

paper towels
sharp cooking knife
cutting board
sealable plastic bag
small mixing bowl
mixing spoon
grilling skewers
grilling tongs

STEPS

1. Thaw the shrimp by putting them in cool water for a few minutes. Drain and pat them dry with paper towels.

2. Cut off the tails of the shrimp and discard them. Then put the shrimp in the sealable plastic bag.

3. Mix together the olive oil, lime juice, cumin, cilantro, salt, and pepper in the bowl to make a marinade.

4. Add the marinade to the plastic bag and seal shut. Shake the bag to coat the shrimp with the marinade. Place in the refrigerator and allow to sit for about 1 hour.

5. Take out the shrimp and slide them onto the grilling skewers.

6. Grill the shrimp over high heat for 1 to 2 minutes on each side.

7. Place the tortillas on the grill for a few seconds to heat them up.

8. Remove the shrimp and tortillas from the grill. Build your tacos using whatever toppings you like. Shredded cabbage, tomatoes, sour cream, and avocados are tasty choices.

DID YOU KNOW?

A lot of people are very allergic to shrimp and other shellfish. Make sure no one at your table is allergic before serving up shrimp tacos.

STEAK KABOBS

MAKES 8 KABOBS

What's better than a good steak? Steak on a stick! These marinated steak kabobs are juicy, delicious, and fun to make. Just cut up some steak and veggies, slide them on a skewer, and toss them on the grill for a full meal on a stick.

INGREDIENTS

1 1/2 tablespoons honey
1 1/2 tablespoons soy sauce
1 tablespoon olive oil
1/4 teaspoon salt
1 pound of beef steak
1 large sweet onion
1 medium-size sweet green bell pepper
1 pound small red potatoes
1 (8-ounce) package fresh mushrooms

EQUIPMENT

small mixing bowl
whisk
sharp cooking knife
cutting board
sealable plastic bag
8 grilling skewers
grilling tongs

STEPS

1. Whisk the honey, soy sauce, olive oil, and salt together in the small bowl to make a marinade.

2. Cut the steak into 1 inch (2.5 cm) cubes. Place the meat in the sealable bag. Pour the marinade over the meat. Seal the bag and shake it to coat the meat. Allow the meat to sit in marinade for 30 minutes or more.

3. Cut the onion into 1/2-inch (1.3-cm) wide wedges.

4. Cut the green pepper into 1-inch (2.5 cm) pieces.

5. Cut the potatoes in half or into 1-inch (2.5 cm) thick pieces.

6. Heat the grill to about 375° F. Remove meat from marinade and dispose of remaining liquid.

7. Slide the pieces of meat and vegetables onto the skewers in this order: beef, onion, potato, mushroom, and pepper. Repeat until skewer is full, then do the same with the rest of the skewers.

8. Place the kabobs on the grill. Cook for 6 to 10 minutes on each side, or until steak is cooked through.

Try This!

Place the skewers in a grill basket to make flipping the kabobs a breeze. This will also help keep the ingredients from falling off the skewers and into the grill.

TWICE-GRILLED PIZZA

MAKES 4-6 SERVINGS

Who doesn't love pizza? Make your next pizza party amazing by lighting up the grill and cooking it in your backyard. This pizza has the same melty cheese, awesome sauce, and crisp crust that you love, but with the added smoky flavors of the grill.

INGREDIENTS

1 pre-made, 12 inch (30.5 cm) pizza crust
olive oil or vegetable oil
1 jar pizza sauce
1 package (8 ounces) shredded mozzarella cheese
toppings such as chopped onions, peppers, pepperoni,
   cooked sausage, ham, or mushrooms
grated Parmesan cheese
Italian seasoning

EQUIPMENT

basting brush
cooking tongs
cutting board
rubber spatula or
   cooking spoon
pizza cutter

STEPS

1 Preheat the grill on high heat for about 10 minutes.

2 Lightly brush oil on both sides of the pizza crust.

3 Reduce the heat on the grill to low. Grill the crust for 1 to 2 minutes per side. Place crust on the side of the grill away from the flames.

4 Remove the crust and place on cutting board. Spread the pizza sauce on top of the crust.

5 Cover the sauce with half of the mozzarella cheese, and then add any toppings you like.

6 Spread the rest of the mozzarella cheese over the toppings. Then sprinkle the pizza with Parmesan cheese and Italian seasoning to taste.

Tip: It's tempting to pile on the toppings, but too much can make the pizza soggy and difficult to cook. Go light and you'll get perfect pizza every time.

7 Place the pizza back on the grill away from the flames and cook for 8 to 10 minutes with the lid closed. When the cheese has melted and begins to brown, the pizza is done.

8 Remove the pizza and allow to cool for 2 minutes. Then slice it up and enjoy!

FINGER-LICKIN' BARBEQUE RIBS

MAKES 3-4 SERVINGS

When you're ready to challenge your grilling skills, be sure to give these mouthwatering ribs a try. Tender, melt-in-your-mouth ribs can be hard to get right. But with this recipe, you're sure to wow your friends and family with a tasty feast.

INGREDIENTS

1 tablespoon ground cumin
1 tablespoon chili powder
1 tablespoon paprika
1 tablespoon garlic powder
2 tablespoons salt
1 tablespoon black pepper
3 pounds of baby back pork ribs
1 cup of your favorite barbeque sauce

EQUIPMENT

small mixing bowl
mixing spoon
paper towels
butter knife or spoon
aluminum foil
rib rack
meat thermometer
basting brush

STEPS

1 In the small bowl, stir together the cumin, chili powder, paprika, garlic powder, salt, and pepper to make a dry rub.

2 Wash the ribs with warm water and then pat dry with paper towels.

3 Peel the silver membrane off the back side of the ribs. Slide a butter knife or spoon under the membrane to get hold of it. Removing this membrane helps the flavors of the spices and smoke from the grill to better penetrate the meat.

4 Sprinkle 3 to 4 tablespoons of the dry rub mix on each side of the ribs. Then rub the spices into the meat.

5 Cover the grate of the grill with aluminum foil. This will help to spread out the heat and catch the drippings to prevent flare-ups as the ribs cook.

6 Heat grill to about 225° F (107° C). Place a "smoke bomb" on the grill grate over the flames (see page 7).

7 Place the ribs in the rib rack, and then put the rack on the foil over the grill grate.

8 Cook the ribs on low heat for 2 to 3 hours. Do not open lid during this time to keep in the heat and smoke.

9 Check the ribs. The meat may look ready to eat, but use a meat thermometer to be sure. The internal temperature should be 180° F (82° C). If it isn't, continue cooking for another hour or until the meat reaches the correct temperature.

10 Remove the ribs and set aside. Remove the foil from the grill and turn the heat to high.

11 Place ribs back on grill grate and brush both sides with your favorite barbecue sauce. Cook over high heat for 2 to 3 minutes on each side until the sauce begins to caramelize.

12 Remove ribs and place on cutting board. Allow to rest for 4 to 5 minutes, then carefully cut them into individual servings. Now grab lots of napkins and dig in!

Try This!

If you like sweeter ribs, add 2 to 3 tablespoons of brown sugar to the dry rub mix.

GRILLED BANANA BOATS

MAKES 4 BANANA BOATS

You've already cooked up awesome burgers, ribs, and veggies. Now it's time for dessert. Wait . . . dessert on the grill? Why not? These chocolaty, grilled banana boats will make you feel like you're at a camp out! This twist on the classic banana split is surprisingly delicious and a lot of fun to make.

INGREDIENTS

4 large yellow bananas
4 tablespoons chocolate chips
4 tablespoons chopped nuts
1/2 cup miniature marshmallows
vanilla ice cream

EQUIPMENT

sharp cooking knife
cutting board
aluminum foil
cooking tongs

STEPS

1. Cut a long slit along the inside curve of each banana. Do not cut all the way through.

2. Wrap aluminum foil partially around each banana to form a "boat."

3. Spread the slit open to make a pocket in the banana. Fill the pocket with chocolate chips, nuts, and marshmallows.

4. Place the banana boats on the grill. Cook on low heat for 8 to 10 minutes or until the chocolate is melted and the marshmallows begin to brown.

5. Remove from grill and allow to cool for a few minutes before serving with the ice cream.

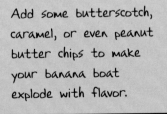

Try This!

Add some butterscotch, caramel, or even peanut butter chips to make your banana boat explode with flavor.

GRILLED DONUT ICE CREAM SANDWICHES

MAKES 4 DONUT DESSERTS

Here's something for people who have a serious sweet tooth. If you're in the mood for something gooey and sweet, these amazing grilled donut treats should hit the spot. It only takes a few minutes, so be sure to make enough to share!

INGREDIENTS

4 glazed donuts
vanilla ice cream
chocolate sauce
whipped cream
maraschino cherries

EQUIPMENT

sharp cooking knife
cutting board
grilling spatula
serving plates
ice cream scoop

STEPS

1. Slice the donuts in half horizontally.

2. Grill the donuts on high heat for 1 to 2 minutes on each side. Then remove and place on separate plates.

3. Serve by placing a scoop of ice cream between two grilled donut halves.

4. Now make your dessert a masterpiece! Top the donuts off with a drizzle of chocolate sauce, a big dollop of whipped cream, and a maraschino cherry.

Try This!

Make this dessert truly amazing by adding some grilled pineapple slices. Sprinkle pineapple slices with some brown sugar and cinnamon. Then grill over medium heat for 2 to 3 minutes on each side. Add a pineapple slice to each donut before adding the ice cream.

READ MORE

Cook, Deanna F. *Cooking Class: 57 Fun Recipes Kids Will Love to Make (and Eat!).* North Adams, Mass.: Storey Publishing, 2015.

Jorgensen, Katrina. *Football Tailgating Recipes: Tasty Treats for the Stadium Crowd.* Football Cookbooks. North Mankato, Minn.: Capstone Press, 2015.

Wagner, Lisa. *Cool Backyard Grilling: Beyond the Basics for Kids Who Cook.* Minneapolis: ABDO Publishing Company, 2014.

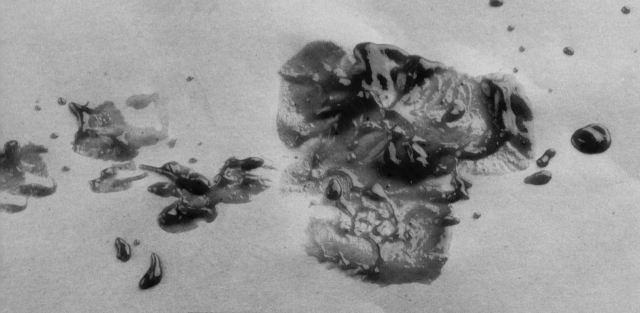

INTERNET SITES

FactHound offers a safe, fun way to find Internet sites related to this book. All of the sites on Facthound have been researched by our staff.

Here's all you do:
Visit *www.facthound.com*
Type in this code: 9781515738152

 Check out projects, games and lots more at
www.capstonekids.com

$27.99

10-17